Irish
JOKES

Published in the UK by
POWERFRESH Limited
21 Rothersthorpe Crescent
Northampton
NN4 8JD

Telephone   0845 130 4565
Facsimile   0845 130 4563
E Mail   info@powerfresh.co.uk

Copyright ' 2003
Cover and interior layout by Powerfresh
Illustrations Sanjit Saha

ISBN 190292939X

Printed in Malta by Gutenberg Press Ltd
Powerfresh April 2003

An Irish Farmer comes into some, money and decides to join this swishy social club in Britain. The cost per entry are astronomical but it's got every amenity possible in it's leisure complex as well as hunting facilities. He gets on fine for a week or two but after that time one of the directors says he wants to have a word with him.

'I'm afraid some of our members are unhappy with your behaviour' he says to Paddy.

'In what way?' Paddy asks, bewildered.

'Well for one thing,' the director says, 'When you're out hunting the expression we use is 'After the fox,' and not, 'Chase. the fuckin' bastard.'

'Is that all?' asks Paddy.

'No, we don't like you piddling in the swimming pool either.'

Paddy decides to take a stand on this one.

'I beg your pardon' he says, 'I saw one of your other members piddling in the pool only yesterday.'

'Maybe so' the director replies, 'but hardly from the top of the diving board.'

Mick got a job as a porter in a big hotel in New York.

One day he was standing at the front door when an American said to him, 'Hey Mick, be an angel and run up to Room 273 and see if I left my pyjamas and razor on the bed. I'm rushing to the airport and my plane leaves in ten minutes. Five minutes later, Mick comes running down the stairs and says to the American, 'You're right. Both of them are on the bed.'

Did, you hear about the Irishman. who gave back the bowling balls because they had holes in them?

How do you recognise an Irish firing squad? They stand in a circle.

Ireland has just produced an Evel Kinevel style daredevil. His latest stunt is trying to jump over thirty motorbikes in a bus.

A PICTURE OF DUBLIN AT NIGHT

The phone rings while Paddy is in the bath and he gets out to answer it.

'Hello, is that Seamus?'

'No, this is Paddy.'

'I must have the wrong number then. Sorry for disturbing you.'

'It's all right. I had to answer the phone anyway.'

Irish foreman to labourer applying for a job on a building site: 'I can't give you a start today because I have a fellow in your job that didn't come in. If he doesn't come in again tomorrow I'll send him home and you can start the job that he didn't finish.'

The old Irish farmer is dying and his wife is sitting by the bed with her four sons. Three of them are burly lads but the fourth one is a skinny little runt, and not at all like the others.

'I have to know before I die,' the farmer says to his wife, 'if that little boy is mine. It's been torturing me all my life that he isn't but I couldn't ask you till now.'

'I swear to God he is,' the woman says, and the next moment the man dies.

His wife then breathes a sigh of relief and says, 'Thanks be to Christ he didn't ask me about the other three.'

An Irish mother wrote this to her son: We went to Ballybunion for a week this summer and it only rained twice, the first time for three days and the second time for four days.

Your father has a great new job where he is over five hundred men, he's cutting the grass in the local cemetery.

Your Aunt Mary has just had her appendix taken out and a new washing machine installed.

Your Uncle Tom, the one who drank ten glasses of liver salts every day for the last forty years, died last week. We had to beat his liver to death with a stick.

The people next door are keeping pigs in their backyard. We only got wind of it yesterday.

Your Uncle Frank who works in the brewery was drowned last week in a big vat of beer. He didn't have a painful death though because he got out three times to go to the gents.

There was once an Irish funeral which was cancelled because of a strike. Eventually it took place though. They managed to recruit a skeleton staff.

Have you heard about the Irishman who said he would die happy if he could only live to see his own funeral?

An undertaker called to a client's house on the day of a funeral asking his widow, 'Excuse me, ma'am, but would this be where the dead man lives?'

When an Irishman was asked to define winter, he expostulated in beautifully bullish fashion, 'It's the time of year when it gets late early.'

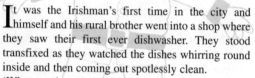

It was the Irishman's first time in the city and himself and his rural brother went into a shop where they saw their first ever dishwasher. They stood transfixed as they watched the dishes whirring round inside and then coming out spotlessly clean.

'Whoever invented that contraption was a clever man,' said the first brother.

'Aye' agreed the second, 'and a lazy bastard!'

Why did the Irishman kill himself? He wanted to get revenge on the Samaritans for taking him off their danger list.

An Irishman, and Englishman and a Scotsman fell off a roof. Which reached the ground first? The Scotsman. The Irishman got lost and the Englishman stopped to ask directions.

How can an Irishman tell if his wife is dead? The sex is the same, but the dishes are piled up in the sink.

Paddy is in bed with his girlfriend. Just as he's about to ejaculate she says, 'Maybe we should be careful; I'm not taking anything.

'Now let's get one thing straight,' Paddy tells her in no uncertain terms, 'The only thing I ever pulled out of was bad digs.'

When Mickey heard that the new girl in the office was a lesbian, he asked her: 'Exactly what part of Lesbia are you from?'

Irishman on his twin brother: 'Begod, sure Seamus is so like me I often mistake him for meself.'

How many Irish women does it take to change a lightbulb. None. They all just sit there and say, 'Arrah sure musha aren't we all right here in the dark.'

Then there was the Irishman who thought cunnilingus was an airline...until he discovered Smirnoff.

Irish farms are completely overgrown with undergrowth.

Irishmen think their inferiority complexes aren't as good as anyone else's.

There was once an Irishman who thought fellatio was a character from Shakespeare.

When an Irishman read a news room report that someone in the world was having sex every three seconds he said, 'Jaysus he must be an awful randy bastard.'

Two Irishmen conversing on the street.

First Irishman: 'Have you seen Casey?'
Second Irishman: 'No. I thought I saw a man who looked like him yesterday, and he thought he saw a man who looked like me, but when we got up close we realised it was neither of us.'

W hat would you get if you offered an Irishman a penny for his thoughts?
Change.

What would you call an Irishman who sits in your garden all day?
Patty O'Furniture

An Irishman arranging a date with his girlfriend: 'I'll see you at the bridge. If I'm there first I'll put a notch on the wall and if you're there first, wipe it off again."

Philosophical speculation by an Irishman: 'If my father was alive today he'd be five years dead.'

What's the latest invention on Irish airplanes? Outside toilets.

ADubliner was walking down the road with a
Galway man when he saw an acquaintance
across the street.

'I don't like him,' he confided to his Galway
colleague, 'he called me a Dublin bastard once.'

'Really?' replied the Galwegian, 'and which part of
the insult bothered you?'

If you still don't believe the Irish have a penchant for answering one question with another, sample the following conversation that once took place on a factory phone:

A. Could I speak to your boss, please?

B. Who am I speaking to?

A. Why do you ask?

B. Is that any of your business?

A. So you're not going to tell me?

B. What gives you that impression?

A. Does that mean you ARE going to tell me?

B. Why should I?

A. What reason would be good enough?

B. What do YOU think?

A. Do you really expect me to continue playing these, silly games with you?

B. That depends on you, doesn't it?

A. Oh, so you agree they're silly games do you?

B. I didn't say that did I?

A. What else would you call them?

B. Why don't you tell me?

A. Look are you going to get me the boss or not?

B. Do you not think I'm entitled to know who I'm talking to?

A. Do you not think I'm entitled to speak to your boss?

B. Do you realise this is where we came in?

An Irishman walked into a bar in New York and fell into conversation with another drinker.

After a few moments he said, 'You sound like a Dubliner.'

'I am' the man replied.

'That s amazing' said the other man. 'So am I.'

'What part?'

'North Circular Road.'

'I don't believe it' said the other man, 'That s my native street too.'

'And where do you work?' he continued.

'Arnotts.'

'I don't believe it, so do I.'

At this stage another drinker, hearing the raised voices asked the barman what was going on.

'Oh nothing much,' he said, 'It's just the two Kelly twins having a chat.'

When someone remarked to an Irish widow that her deceased husband looked very happy in his coffin, she explained his expression with customary Irish logic: 'He died in his sleep and doesn't know he's dead yet, but when he wakes up in the morning the shock will probably kill nim.'

Two Irishmen are doing a crossword. 'Old blankety blank had a farm' says one, 'Who's that?'
'Macdonald' replies the other.
'And how do you spell it?'
'E.I.E.I.O.'

Paddy's wife died and he was informed he would have to share the hearse to the graveyard with his mother-in-law. 'Very well' he agreed finally, 'but 'twill spoil the day for me.'

It was Paddy's first day with the Air Corps and he was thrilled skinny.

As he was cruising across the Atlantic, ground control beamed him up a message.

'Give me your height and location,' said a voice.

'I'm five foot nine and I'm sittin' behind the steerin' wheel,' Paddy replied.

ATipperary girl has just won the Miss Ireland contest. Her measurements are 38-22-36. And the same for the other arm.

Said one Irishman to another meeting up with him for the first time in many years. 'I heard a rumour that you died Paddy?' 'I heard that rumour too,' said the other man, 'but it actually turned out to be someone else, much to my relief.'

Did you hear about the fellow who stayed up all night wondering where the sun went? In the morning it dawned on him.

47

There was once an Irishman who left the play at the interval because the programme said Act Two took place 'Two weeks later.'

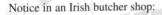

Notice in an Irish butcher shop:

WILL CUSTOMERS PLEASE REFRAIN FROM
SITTING ON THE BACON SLICER, AS WE'RE
GETTING A LITTLE BEHIND WITH OUR
ORDERS.

Paddy was at a lecture on medicine. A renowned surgeon made the pronouncement that the first few moments of a person's life were the most dangerous.

Paddy mused over this for a moment, then commented, 'Yerra,.and the last few can be a bit dodgy too!'

Michael Pat did something disgusting, and his sister said, 'You rascal you. If Mam was alive now she'd turn in her grave.'

Two things Irish people say when they're. annoyed:

1. 'Don't took at me. in that tone. of voice.'

2. 'I'm not even going to bother ignoring that remark.'

This Irish guy attends a shrink for many years. Frustrated finally, the shrink tells him he can cure his depression simply by going on a holiday.

A few weeks later the shrink gets a postcard from the Algarve with this message:

'Having a great time.... Why ?'

This was an Irishman's defence at a court case where he was charged with a reckless display of violence: 'Honest, Your Honour, I didn't mean to hurt him. All I had in me fist was me hand.'

And then there was the fella who wasn't known outside Ireland but was world famous in Waterford.

What do Irish people do when they want to buy houses?
They go to British Home Stores.

Paddy was on his honeymoon but was too shy to sleep with his wife.

'Are you not cold?' she asked, slipping off her clothes as she slid under the covers.

'That I am' said Paddy, growing redder by the minute, 'that I am.'

'You know' said his wife, 'when I was this cold back in Galway, my father used to come in beside me in the bed to keep me warm.'

Paddy thought for a minute.

'Well if you think I'm going all the way back to Galway for your old man you've got another thing comin'.'

It was a perfect Irish marriage: she didn't want to, and he couldn't.

What's an Irish cocktail? A pint of Guinness with a potato in it.

Commit suicide the Irish way: slip arsenic into your tea while you're looking the other way.

Michael Pat went to Canada and saw two lumberjacks using a cross cut saw. He watched them for a while fascinated, and then went over to the taller of the two. 'Look' he said, 'If that little fellow on the other side of the tree wants to use the saw, let him or I'll kick your teeth in.'

The Irishman was on his first parachute jump and was getting instructions. 'Pull the ripcord on the count of ten' said the instructor, 'and if that doesn't work, wait three more seconds and then pull the emergency cord. After you land, a lorry will be waiting for you to take you to the base.'

Paddy does everything he's told, but the ripcord fails him, and so does the emergency cord. 'Be the hokey' he says, 'this isn't my day. I bet the bloody lorry will be late too!'

An Irish farmer found himself with electricity in his house for the first time in his life after coming into some money and he was over the moon about it. 'It's brilliant' he told a friend. 'I just switch on the light and then I have absolutely no problem finding the matches for my candles.'

Did you hear about the health-conscious Irish furniture salesman?
He would only stock decaffeinated coffee tables.

An Irishman always got a pain in his eye everytime he drank tea. After many years, a consultant found the solution to his problem. He told him to take the spoon out after stirring the sugar.

Paddy was born ignorant and he's been losing ground ever since.

In fact the stork who brought him should have been fined for smuggling dope.

He did have an idea once...but it died of loneliness.

Did you hear about the Irish murderer who was sentenced to the electric chair?
He was rather disturbed when they put him sitting in it. 'Are you sure this thing is safe?' he said.

Paddy heard the value of the pound was going down, but that the value of bread was increasing. Now he saves bread.

This Irish boy writes a letter to Santa requesting 'something to wear and something to play with.' Guess what he got? A pair of trousers with the pockets cut out!

How would you recognise an Irish loo?

Incoming traffic has the right of way.

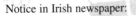

Notice in Irish newspaper:

PIANO FOR SALE ONE OWNER SLIGHTLY CRACKED.

There was once an Irishman who killed all three of his wives and two of them were only napping.

If ignorance is really bliss, why aren't more Irishmen happy?

Two Irishmen are lying in bed together looking rather disgruntled. One say to the other, 'Y'know Mick this wife swappin' lark isn't really all it's cracked up to be.'

The main trouble with Ireland is that every Tom, Dick and Harry is called Paddy.

Did you here about the generous Paddy who gave his ticket to the Marcel Marceau concert to Ray Charles ?

An Irishman who had spent all his life in London was asked if he ever came across anti Irish feeling among the British.

'Not much' he says, 'but the day after I came off the boat I was arrested for hitting a navvy in the elbow with my eyelid.'

An Irishman describes a circle as a big round line with a hole, in the middle.

The naive Irish lad didn't know what to do on the wedding night so he phoned his dad.

'Put the hardest part of yourself where she pees,' he advises.

A few hours later the dad gets another phone call, this time from the bride.

'Could you please tell your son to get his head out of the toilet bowl,' she asks.

Then there was the Irishman who was refused a place on the chess team because of his height.

Don't ever ask an Irishman for street directions. He'll probably tell you, 'Arrah, sure, ye shouldn't be startin' from here.'

What about the Irish farmer who won the Nobel Prize?
He was out standing in his own field.

How many Irishmen does it take to change a lightbulb?

Five. One to put in the bulb, and the other four to turn the ladder.

Pity the poor Irish farmer who gave his hens hot water so they'd lay boiled eggs.

We may describe an Irish gentleman as someone who will hold the door open for his wife while she brings the bins out.

Happiness for an Irishman is being married to a nymymyhomaniac who owns a racecourse above a pub...and who'll turn into a potato after sex.

When Michael Paul's father told him he was buying him an encyclopaedia for school, he said, 'That's very nice of you Daddy, but y'know I think I'd prefer to walk like all the other lads.'

O'Reilly rang up Aer Lingus.

'How long is it to Mexico?' he asked.
'Just a moment' said the receptionist.
'Thanks' he replied, hanging up.

D id you hear about the Irish, queer?

He preferred women to booze.

Paddy told Mike he was intending to sell his old banger of a car.

'Yerra, you won't get much for that jalopy unless you turn the clock back' was Mike's advice.

Paddy took it on board and changed the mileage. A few weeks later, Mike met him on the street and asked him if he'd had any luck getting rid of it.

'Sure what would I want to get rid of it for?' Paddy screamed, 'and there only 2,000 miles on the clock!'

Paddy the Irishman, Paddy the Englishman and Paddy the Scotsman all went on Mastermind with their specialised topics.

The Englishman chose Cricket: 1924-1939 as his theme.

The Scotsman researched Edinburgh History, 1901-1989.

Then it came to Paddy the Irishman's turn. He hadn't read up much, but decided to use all his experience in the clothes shop where he worked.

His topic? Anoraks: £10.99 to £15.99.

Q. Why did the Irish transport official leave the railway gate ajar?
A. He was half-expecting a train.